Sabine Lohf

I MADE IT MYSELF

Sabine Lohf

I MADE IT MYSELF

please give me an answer

ⓅⓅ CHILDRENS PRESS ®
CHICAGO

Translation by Anthea Bell

Library of Congress Cataloging-in-Publication Data

Lohf, Sabine.
   [Das hab ich selbst gemacht.   English]
   I made it myself / by Sabine Lohf.
      p.   cm.
   Translation of: Das hab ich selbst gemacht.
   Summary: Provides instructions on how to make a variety of craft
projects using materials found around the house.
   ISBN 0-516-09254-5
   1. Handicraft—Juvenile literature.   [1. Handicraft.]   I. Title.
TT160.L6413   1989
745.5—dc20   89-22252
                                                            CIP
                                                           AC

Published in the United States in 1990 by Childrens Press®, Inc.,
5440 North Cumberland Avenue, Chicago, IL 60656.

This book is based on contributions published in the German
magazine *Spielen Und Lernen* © Velber Verlag GmbH, Seelze,
F.R.G. This collection was originally published under the title *Das
Hab Ich Selbst Gemacht,* copyright © 1983 by Ravensburger
Buchverlag Otto Maier GmbH, West Germany.

Contents

To make a rag rug, you will need old tights or stockings, bits of old curtains, old shirts, and dresses, and anything else suitable you can find. You can also weave raffia, knitting yarn, beads, feathers, and sticks into your rug.

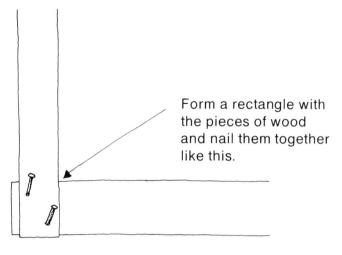

Form a rectangle with the pieces of wood and nail them together like this.

Make the framework for weaving the rug first. You will need four flat pieces of wood, nails and a hammer, and string.

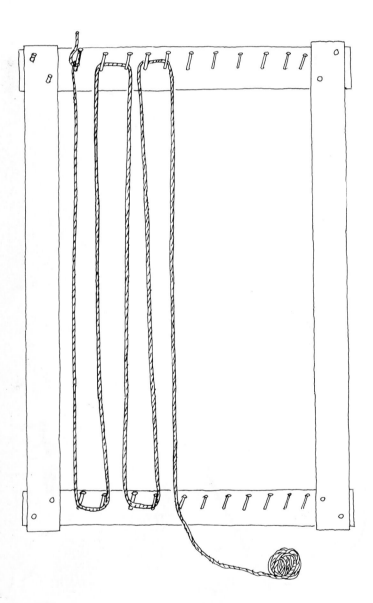

When the pieces of wood are nailed together like a big picture frame, drive a series of nails into the top and bottom sides of the frame. Then tie one end of your string to a corner nail and wind it around the nails as shown in the sketch.

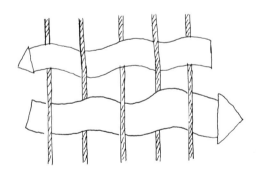

Cut or tear the rags into long strips and weave them under and over the strings, going in the opposite direction on the next row. Go on until you have used up all the rags and the rug is finished.

Rag Rug

This rag rug is as colorful as any Oriental rug, but you can make it with bits and pieces of old rags. Instructions for weaving the rug are on the opposite page.

To make the monsters, you will need: stiff cardboard, a pair of scissors, glue, envelope fasteners, paint, and a brush.

Get someone with strong hands to help you cut the cardboard. It's hard work.

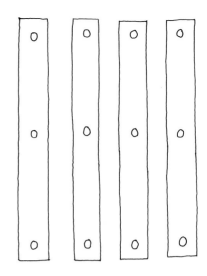

First cut the cardboard into strips. You will need at least four strips for each monster. Bore three holes in each strip.

Now cut out the heads. They will look very fierce if you give them pointed teeth. Paint the heads. Don't forget the monsters' mouths and eyes!

Glue the two halves of each head to two of the cardboard strips, as shown here.

Make the other two cardboard strips into an X shape and place them behind the strips with the head on them, as shown. Fasten with metal envelope fasteners through the holes.

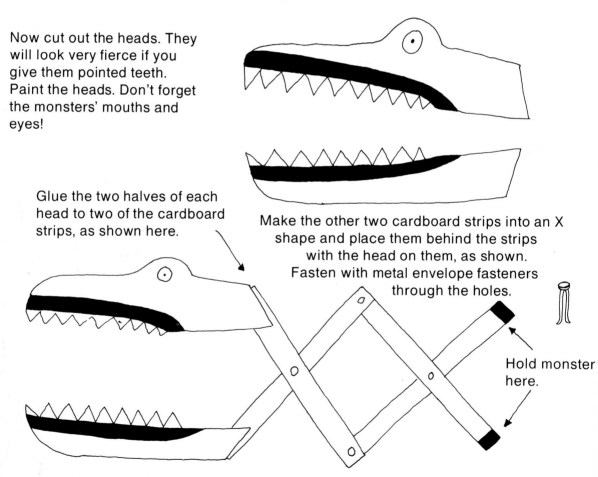

Hold monster here.

Now hold the ends of your monster and move them like scissor handles. You will make the monster's mouth open and shut.

Snip, Snap, and Clack

Snip, Snap, and Clack
are three monsters.
Very useful for chasing
ghosts away—
and you could use them
in a puppet show
or a shadow theater too.

A line with prettily painted clothespins on it is very useful. Once you've got it up, you can pin letters, pictures, or notes to your line.

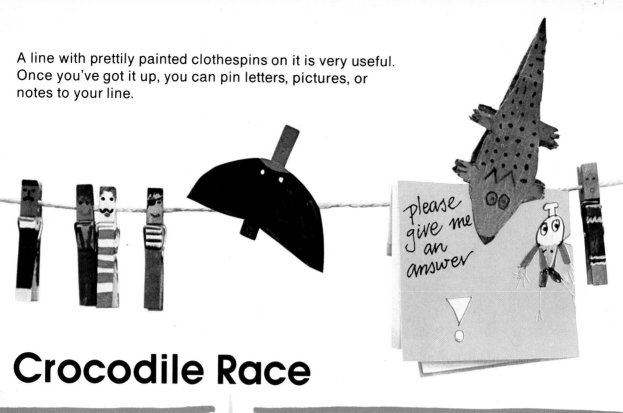

Crocodile Race

First make the crocodiles out of clothespins. Then take a length of string or heavy thread. Fasten one end to the crocodile and the other end to a toothpick.

How to play: draw lines for START and FINISH on a big sheet of paper. At the word "Go" each player begins winding the crocodile's string around the toothpick. First crocodile to cross the finish line is the winner. No pulling —you must wind the string properly!

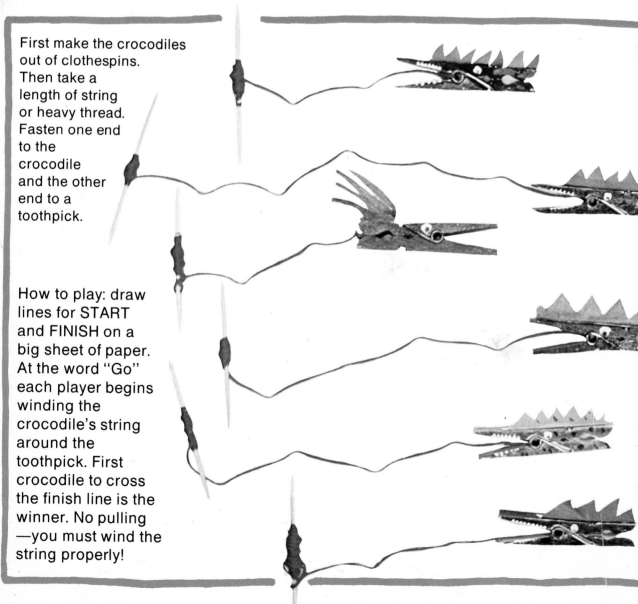

Clothespin Crocodiles

You can make crocodiles and all sorts of other creatures out of ordinary clothespins. You will need: wooden clothespins, paint, paintbrushes, a little cardboard, scraps of yarn, and glue. You can paint the clothespins or glue decorations on them. This page shows some ideas. You can probably think of lots more.

Tape the construction paper around the 6-inch circle of cardboard to make a round box.

You will need a circle of thick cardboard 6 inches in diameter, a strip of construction paper 2 inches wide and about 19 inches long, a cardboard tube from inside a roll of paper towels, a rectangular box, a toothpick, thin cardboard, a pencil, paints and paintbrushes, thin wire, clear tape, and a nail for boring holes.

Cut a circle out of thin cardboard and tape it over one end of the paper-towel tube. ➞

Fold a piece of thin cardboard to make steps.

Put a toothpick through the center of the round box.

The square box makes a base for the merry-go-round.

Then fix the toothpick to the closed end of the paper-towel tube so that the round box will still turn.

Bore holes around the sides of the box.

Cut figures out of cardboard, paint them bright colors, and fix them to the round box.

Put wire through the figures and fasten it to the holes in the sides of the round box.

Tape the merry-go-round firmly to its base, glue the steps in place, and now your figures can go for rides on the merry-go-round.

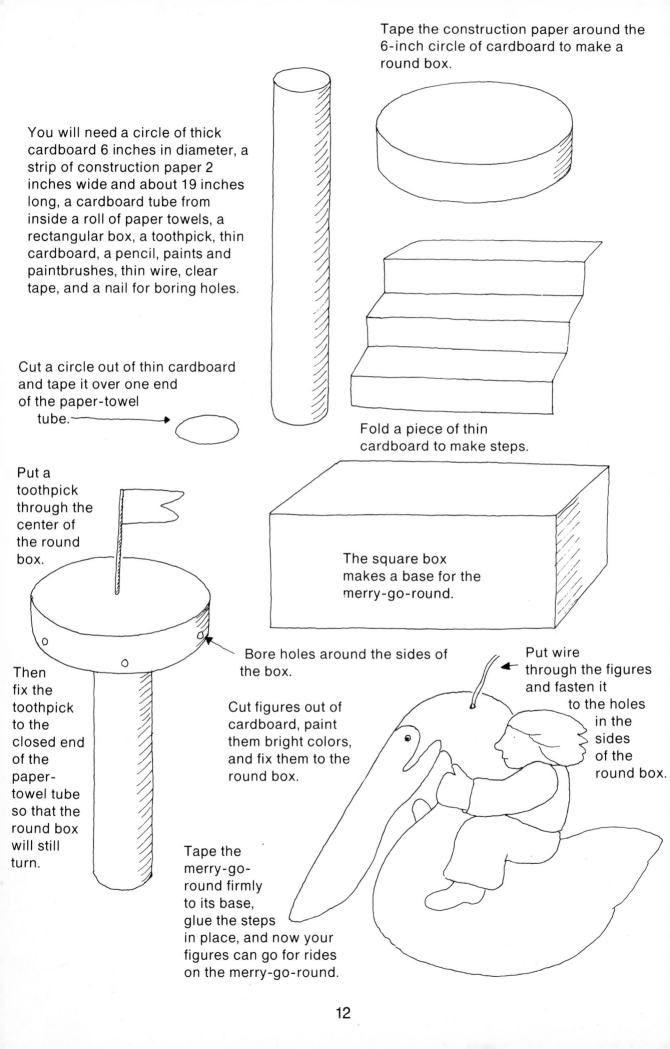

Merry-Go-Round

Here's a merry-go-round with funny figures that really goes around—you can easily make it in an afternoon. It's quite simple. For instructions, see the opposite page.

You will need: heavy cardboard, scissors, glue, elastic, paints and paintbrushes, a little colored paper or scraps of yarn.

Cover the dotted section with glue.

First cut a circle out of heavy cardboard. Make a cut in it along the dotted line. Put the cut surfaces together and glue in place. Weight the cardboard down until the glue is dry.

Side view of the mask when glue is dry.

When your basic mask is ready, cut holes for the eyes and bore small holes at the sides to take a length of elastic, so that you can wear the mask. Thread elastic through the holes.

You can make all sorts of different masks from the basic circle:

You can make beaks or noses out of a quarter circle of cardboard. Cut it out and glue the edges together.

with ears,

with hair,

with a beak.

Once you have learned the trick of it, you'll soon have lots of ideas for making other masks of your own.

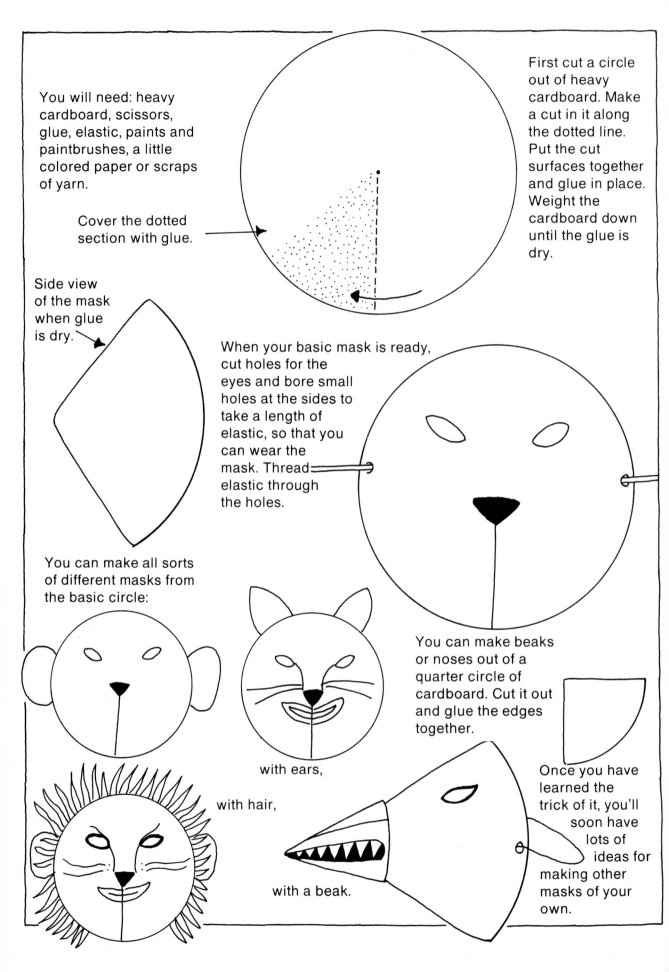

Party Masks

The lion wasn't going to come to the party because he said he didn't have his mane stuck on properly yet—so then his friends put it right. Now the party can begin! Here are masks for a cat, a mouse, a bird, and a fierce dragon as well as the lion. Why not make masks and have a party of your own?

You will need: a cardboard carton big enough to go over your head, the tubes from inside two rolls of toilet paper for the horns, cardboard for the ears, scissors, glue, paint and brushes. Then you can begin to make the cow's head. It's much simpler than it may look.

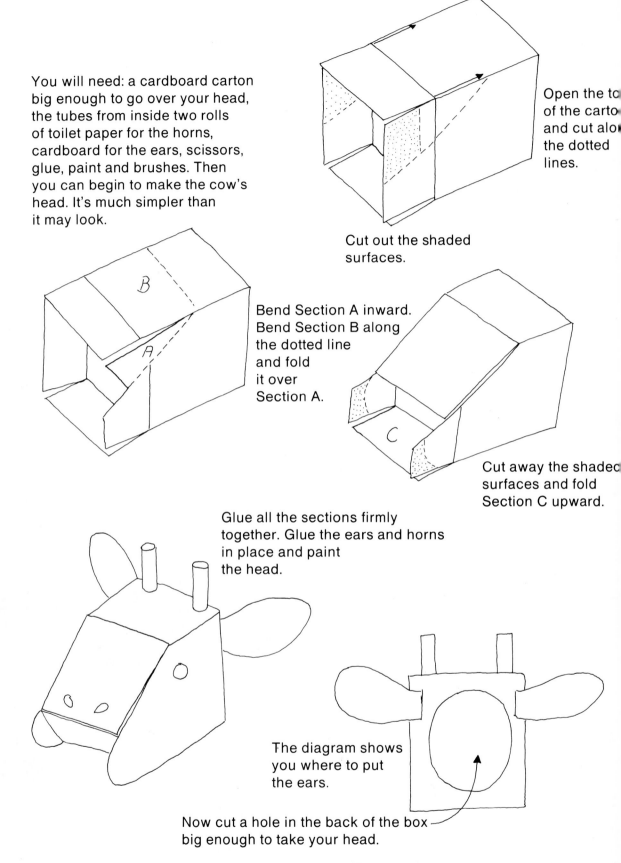

Open the top of the carton and cut along the dotted lines.

Cut out the shaded surfaces.

Bend Section A inward. Bend Section B along the dotted line and fold it over Section A.

Cut away the shaded surfaces and fold Section C upward.

Glue all the sections firmly together. Glue the ears and horns in place and paint the head.

The diagram shows you where to put the ears.

Now cut a hole in the back of the box big enough to take your head.

(CAUTION: Do not run while wearing the mask. Use it only for blindman's buff. If you want to wear the mask for other games or to wear it outdoors, cut eyeholes in it large enough so that you can see well.)

A Cardboard Cow

This cardboard cow's head has no holes for the eyes— you can use it in a game of blindman's buff instead of a blindfold. Try it for a game with a difference! The cow may not be able to see, but she's very good at hearing and smelling things.

To make seven bowling pins, you will need: seven empty plastic bottles, newspaper, glue, scissors, a funnel and a little sand, paints and brushes, scraps of fabric, yarn, and colored paper.

Cut or tear newspaper into strips.

Crumple up a double sheet of newspaper to make a ball for each figure's head, leaving a little paper at the bottom of the ball for the neck.

Glue the newspaper strips all over the crumpled ball to make a firm head.

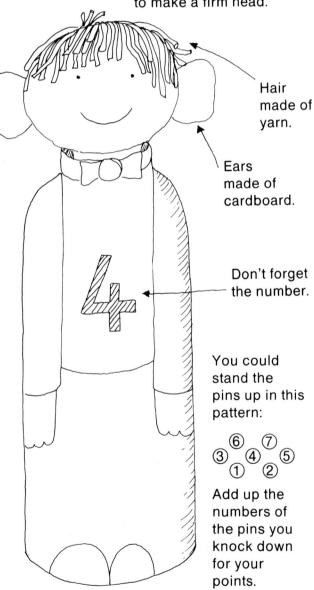

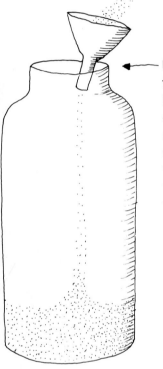

Using a funnel, fill each plastic bottle about one-third full of sand. The sand keeps them from falling over too easily.

Hair made of yarn.

Ears made of cardboard.

Don't forget the number.

You could stand the pins up in this pattern:

⑥ ⑦
③ ④ ⑤
① ②

Add up the numbers of the pins you knock down for your points.

When the sand is in the bottle, place the figure's head in the bottle neck. Paint the figures and decorate them with yarn, fabric, or paper. Paint a number on each figure. The figure with the highest number could have a crown and be King of the Pins.

Stand the pins up, get a ball, and try to knock them over by rolling the ball at them.

Bowling Game

These bowling pins are made of empty plastic bottles, with newspaper heads. You can play with them anywhere—indoors or out-of-doors, on the beach, or in the playground.

Suggestions for Games

First of all find some people to play with you. As well as the houses you have made, you'll need a notepad, a pencil, and some little rubber balls. Stand the houses in a semicircle. Each player must try to roll a ball into the same house three times running. Use House 1 for the first round, House 2 for the second round, and so on. Go on playing until everyone has had three tries at all the houses. Whenever a player rolls a ball into a house, it scores one point. Write the points down and see who has the most at the end of the game.

Or you could try rolling the balls blindfolded. Everyone has three tries, and the numbers of the houses into which the balls roll are written down. Add the points up at the end of the game to see who has won. Perhaps you can think of some more games of your own.

To make the houses, you will need: empty cardboard cartons, scissors, glue, paints, and brushes.

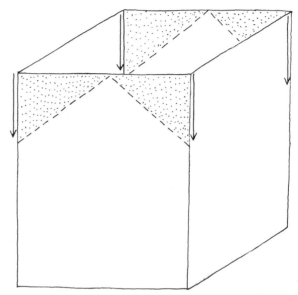

Cut the carton down the lines marked by arrows. Cut away the shaded sections.

Fold the top part of the sides inward along the dotted line. Put some glue on the edges.

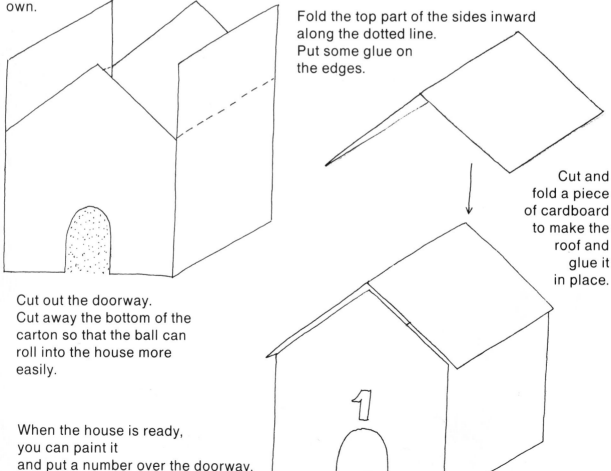

Cut out the doorway. Cut away the bottom of the carton so that the ball can roll into the house more easily.

When the house is ready, you can paint it and put a number over the doorway.

Cut and fold a piece of cardboard to make the roof and glue it in place.

Little Houses

The little houses don't have doors, only doorways, so that you can roll balls into them. See the opposite page for instructions to tell you how to make the houses and suggestions for some games you can play with them.

Why not make a poultry yard?
You will need:
blown eggshells, colored paper,
cardboard, scissors, glue,
paints and brushes.

1. Blow the eggs:
make small holes at the top and
bottom of each egg, hold the eggs
over a bowl, and blow hard.

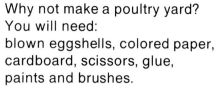

2. Cut out all the parts shown here from colored
paper, cutting each part out several times.

Comb for hens

Larger comb
for rooster

Tail for hens

Beak

This part
goes under
the beak.

Lots of colored
tail feathers
for rooster

Fold all parts
along the dotted lines
and glue to the
eggshells.

Wing →

You could make a few bushes
for the poultry yard too.
Cut them out of card
board and pain
them green. Fold
at the bottom a
shown, and
the bushe
wi
stand
up

Cut a strip of cardboard,
roll it up, and glue the
edges
together.

Put a paper clip
over the glued edges
to help them stick
better.

Foot

Glue the rolled cardboard
on the chicken's foot.

Now put
the eggshel
on top of th
rolled cardboard,
and the chicken is
finished.

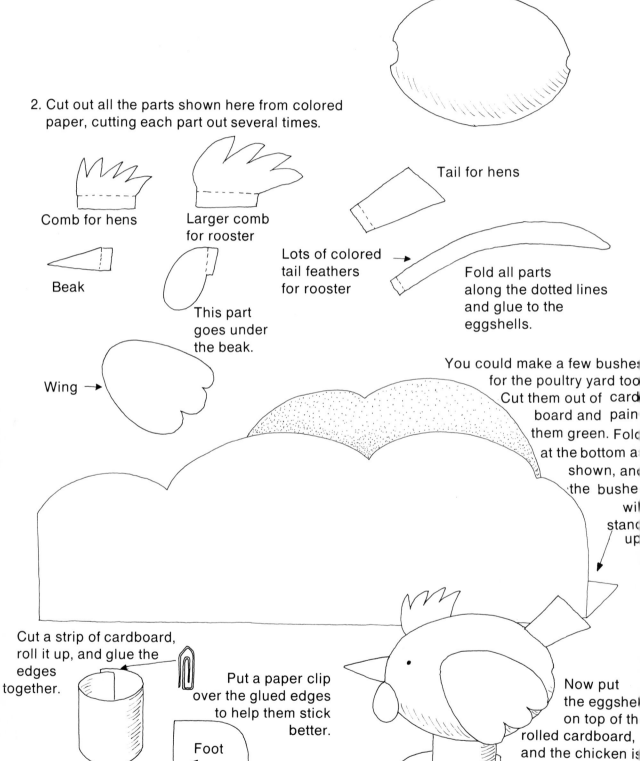

Poultry Yard

What about a poultry yard with a
rooster and several hens to decorate
the table on Easter? See the
opposite page for instructions for
making the chickens.

To make the chicken, you will need a shoe box without its lid, some thin cardboard, scissors, glue, and colored paper.

Stand the shoe box upside down.

Paint two chicken shapes on thin cardboard. Make them the same length as the shoe box at the base.

Cut out the two chicken shapes and glue one to each long side of the shoe box. Cut three openings at the bottom of the chicken.

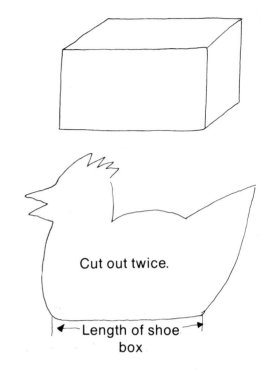

Cut out twice.

← Length of shoe → box

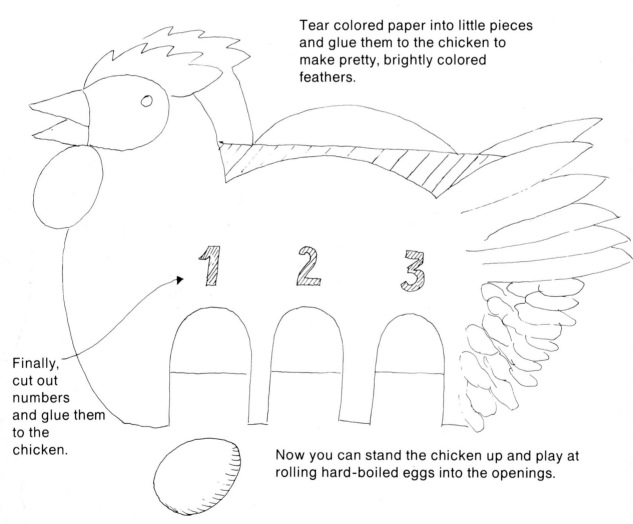

Tear colored paper into little pieces and glue them to the chicken to make pretty, brightly colored feathers.

Finally, cut out numbers and glue them to the chicken.

Now you can stand the chicken up and play at rolling hard-boiled eggs into the openings.

Easter Chicken

This big Easter chicken is made from a shoe box and a little thin cardboard. You can play at rolling Easter eggs through the numbered openings. See who scores the most points. Or you could play the same game with table-tennis balls.

To make the Cackling Chickens, you will need: empty tin cans without sharp edges (e.g., coffee cans), thin cardboard, poster paint, brushes, glue, thin string, rosin (get it from a music store), a nail and a hammer to make a hole in the can. Now follow the diagrams on this page.

Paint the can.

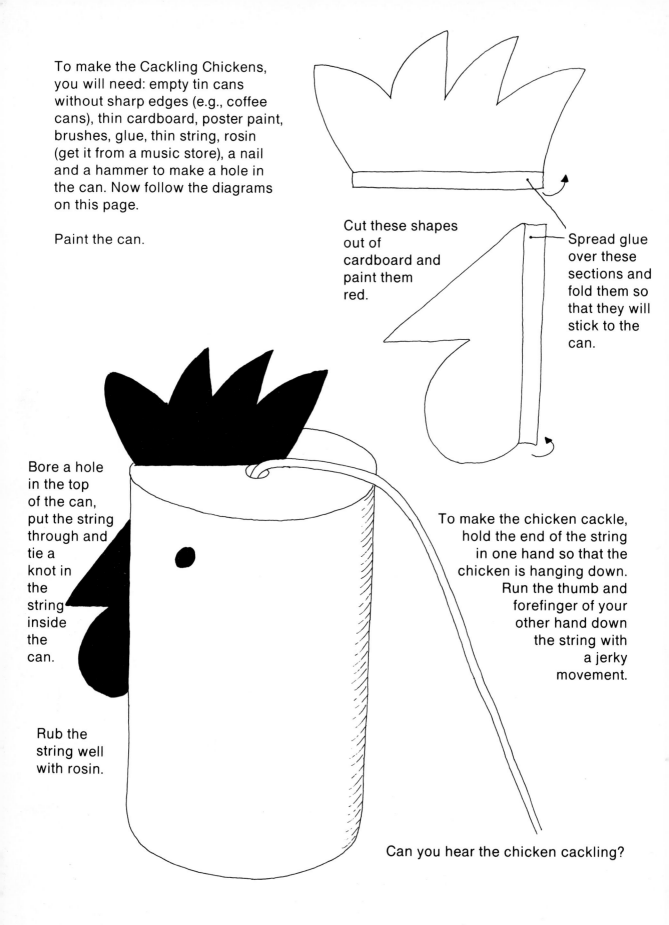

Cut these shapes out of cardboard and paint them red.

Spread glue over these sections and fold them so that they will stick to the can.

Bore a hole in the top of the can, put the string through and tie a knot in the string inside the can.

Rub the string well with rosin.

To make the chicken cackle, hold the end of the string in one hand so that the chicken is hanging down. Run the thumb and forefinger of your other hand down the string with a jerky movement.

Can you hear the chicken cackling?

Cackling Chickens

These chickens really do cackle!
They look amusing hung up by a window
at Easter, too. See the opposite page for
instructions for making them and getting
them to cackle.

What Sort of Eggs Are These?

Strawberry Egg

Mouse Egg

This egg could be a Clock Egg. How would you make it?

Lemon Egg

Ladybug Egg

Mosquito Egg

Plum Egg

Roly-Poly People

You can make little stand-up people who won't lie down out of eggs. Working carefully, make a hole at the top of each egg, just big enough to let the raw egg out. Tip the contents of the egg into a bowl, wash the shell out with water, and let it dry. Drop a little glue into the egg, then put a few ball bearings inside the shell too—just enough to weight the egg down. When the ball bearings are firmly stuck inside the shell, you can paint the egg like a little person and stick hair or a hat on top of the head.

You will need:
a piece of heavy cardboard for
the base, some corrugated
cardboard, glue, paints, a
paintbrush, some pins, a
marble for playing the game.

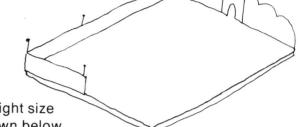

Cut strips of corrugated cardboard to the right size
and glue them to the base in the maze shown below.

You will find it helpful to paint the pattern
on the base first. Then spread glue over
the bottom of the corrugated cardboard
strips. Use pins to fasten the walls of the
maze together. Cut the bushes and light-
house in the background out of a strip of
cardboard and glue them in place. When
the glue has set, you can paint the maze.
To play the maze game, pick the board up
and guide the marble through the maze to
the lighthouse, gently tilting and shaking
the game.

Maze Game

How can the ball get to the light-house? You play the game by picking the board up in both hands and making the marble roll around it until it finds the right way out. There *is* a right way out! Try the game and see.

Collect a few
little stones and
put them together
to make letters
in the sand,
or write
your name
with them.

Games in the Sand

Or you can use stones and little bits
of twig to make funny little people.

Can you find your way
through the maze? Lay some
pebbles out on the sand in
this pattern, and ask your
friends to solve the maze
puzzle.

Ladybug race
Paint some
stones
to look like
ladybugs and
race them down
a track made of
cardboard
propped on a
brick or a box.
Which ladybug
will slide
farthest?
The highest
number wins.

Building a Town

You need only a few pieces of brick, stone,
or concrete and some paint to make your
own town. A lumberyard may give you
some bits of broken brickwork free if
you ask politely. Paint your building
materials in bright colors and use them
to build a town in the sand.

You will need: newspaper, stapler, clear tape, paints, and paintbrushes.

1. First make the handle. Put 5 double sheets of newspaper on top of each other and roll them up diagonally. Fasten the ends with clear tape.

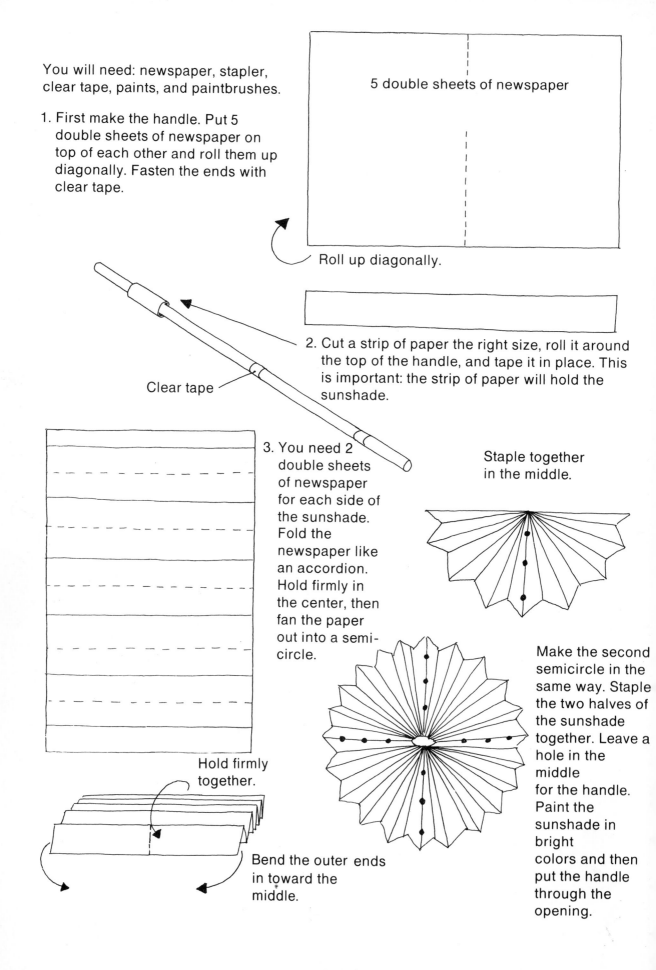

5 double sheets of newspaper

Roll up diagonally.

Clear tape

2. Cut a strip of paper the right size, roll it around the top of the handle, and tape it in place. This is important: the strip of paper will hold the sunshade.

3. You need 2 double sheets of newspaper for each side of the sunshade. Fold the newspaper like an accordion. Hold firmly in the center, then fan the paper out into a semi-circle.

Staple together in the middle.

Make the second semicircle in the same way. Staple the two halves of the sunshade together. Leave a hole in the middle for the handle. Paint the sunshade in bright colors and then put the handle through the opening.

Hold firmly together.

Bend the outer ends in toward the middle.

Sunshades

These sunshades are made of folded newspaper, painted nice bright colors. If you put several sunshades up in the sand and lie under them, it's almost like being in a tent.

You will need:
empty milk cartons,
straws, colored
paper, little empty
boxes, some cotton
(for the steamship),
paints, brushes,
glue, and clear tape
(for the ship made of
straws).

1. Put a milk carton down on a firm surface
and cut away the shaded side. Use a knife.

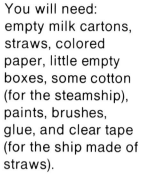

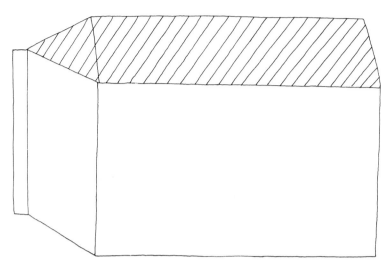

2. Cut a sail out of a piece
of colored paper and put a straw
through it for the mast.

Make a cut at the
bottom of the straw and
fold the two halves
back.

Then you
can glue
the straw
to the
bottom of
the milk
carton.

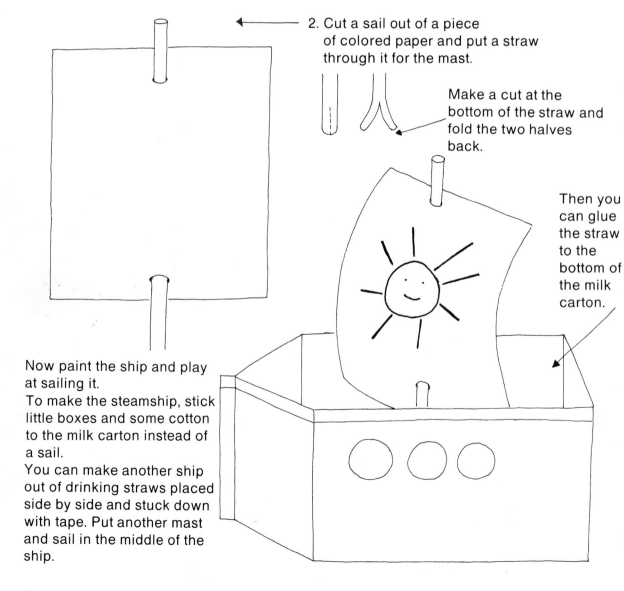

Now paint the ship and play
at sailing it.
To make the steamship, stick
little boxes and some cotton
to the milk carton instead of
a sail.
You can make another ship
out of drinking straws placed
side by side and stuck down
with tape. Put another mast
and sail in the middle of the
ship.

Milk-Carton Ships

If you get your milk in cartons, you can make a whole fleet of ships like these once you have drunk the milk that came inside them.

You will need:
plenty of empty
matchboxes, some
toothpicks, paper, glue,
paints and a paintbrush,
corks or small rolls of
cardboard.

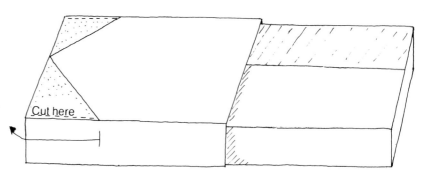

Cut here

Open a matchbox and cut away the dotted
sections of the top of the lid. Turn the lid over and
cut the bottom of the lid to the same shape. This
makes the pointed bow of the ship.

Make a paper flag.
Use a toothpick
for the
flagstaff.

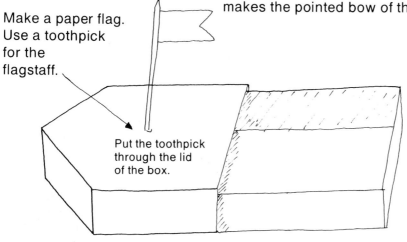

Put the toothpick
through the lid
of the box.

Spread glue on the
edges of the boxes
before folding them
in and sticking them
together.

You can make really long ships
out of several opened matchboxes
fitted together.

Fasten sails, funnels made out of corks,
and more matchboxes
to the ships.

Add a second
opened matchbox
to the first.

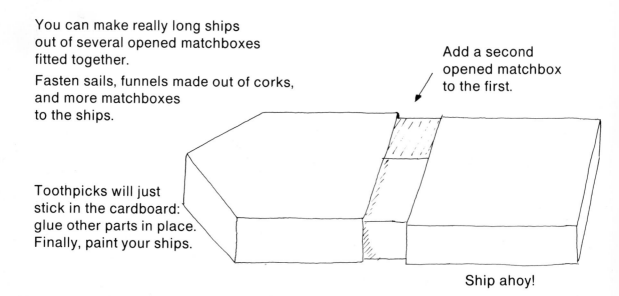

Toothpicks will just
stick in the cardboard:
glue other parts in place.
Finally, paint your ships.

Ship ahoy!

Mini-Steamships

You can float these matchbox steamships in a wading pool or a puddle. They are simple to make, so you can easily have a whole fleet. Ship ahoy!

To make the raft, you will need:
sticks, string, a big darning
needle, a scrap of fabric, paint
and a paintbrush.

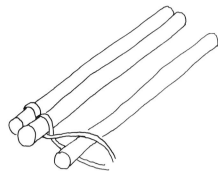

Put 8 sticks of about
the same size side
by side and tie
them together with
string, winding the
string firmly around
them and crossing it
after each stick, as
shown.

When the 8 sticks are tied
together, tie 2 more sticks
crosswise underneath
them.

Place a stick in
the middle of the
raft for the mast,
wind string around
the top of the mast,
and tie the string
to the 4 corners
of the raft.

Make a sail out of a
scrap of fabric and 2 small
sticks. Use a big darning
needle to sew the fabric
in place around the sticks.
You could paint the
sail too.

Tie the sail to
the mast.

Now the raft
can start
its voyage.

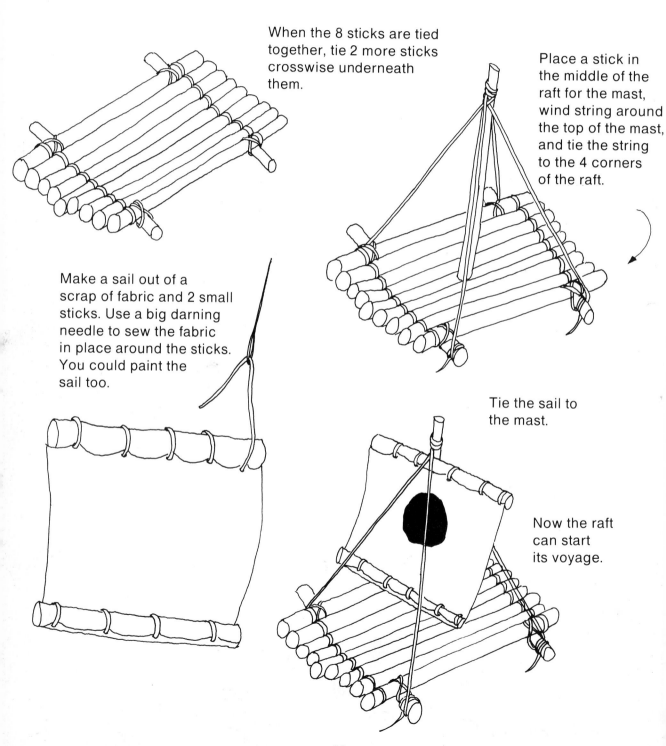

Sailing Raft

Off goes this little raft on a long voyage, pitting itself against the wind and the waves. Where will it come ashore? Robinson Crusoe's island, maybe? Or New York harbor? Build your own raft and send it out on an adventurous journey!

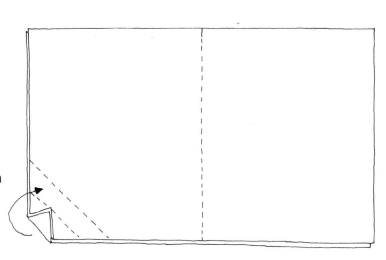

To make the sandals, you
will need: newspaper, glue,
clear tape, and a stapler.

1. Place 2 double sheets of
   newspaper on top of each
   other and fold into a strip
   about 1 inch wide.

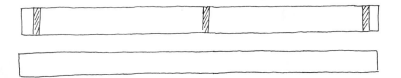

To make 2 sandals, you will
need 3-4 long strips and 2
short strips. Fasten the
strips at the ends with
tape so that they don't
come apart.

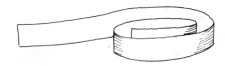

Now wind the strips firmly around
themselves in an oval shape. Tape down the
beginning and end of the wound strips.

Keep on winding the strips until
the oval shape is the size
of your foot.

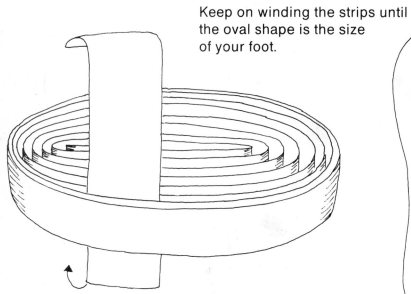

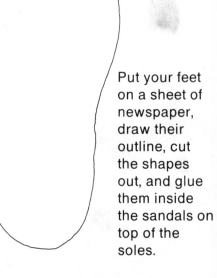

Put your feet
on a sheet of
newspaper,
draw their
outline, cut
the shapes
out, and glue
them inside
the sandals on
top of the
soles.

Push the short strip for the strap through the
outer side of the sole and staple it in place
underneath the sole.

Sandals for Sunny Days

Shoes made of newspaper? Unlikely
as it may sound, this pair is good and
solid. They will last longer than you
might think—they might last right
through summer. But don't go
paddling in these sandals! When
they do fall apart, you can easily
make a new pair.

You will need:
a hammer, nails, screws, wire,
glue, and scraps of wood (ask
a carpenter nicely and he
may give them to you for
nothing, or someone might
saw up some old boards and
planks for you).
Here are some examples of
toys you might make: a little
man, a ship, and a freight train.
You'll be sure to think of more
ideas for yourselves.

(CAUTION: Be careful with the hammer and nails.
Or have an adult do the hammering for you.)

Wooden Toys

Why not see what you can do with a hammer, some nails, and some scraps of wood? You can make your own wooden toys. You could try making a crane, like the one in this picture, or a train like the one shown opposite. Carpentry isn't really difficult, so give it a try.

(CAUTION: Use the rocket only outdoors in an open area. Never point the rocket at your body or at another person.)

If you'd like to build this rocket, you will need: the cardboard tube from a roll of paper towels, some cardboard, paints and a paintbrush, a rubber band, all-purpose glue, a stick measuring about 20 inches.

Cut out a square of thin cardboard. Then cut it along the dotted lines as shown in the diagram so that you end up with 4 triangles.

Make a notch in the top of the stick.

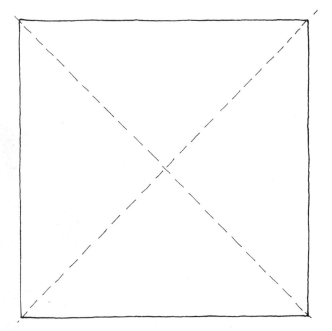

Make four lengthwise cuts in one end of the cardboard tube. Glue the triangles in place in these slits. Cut a strip of cardboard a little longer than the tube. Bore two holes in one end of it.

About 1¼ in.

Assemble the parts like this:

1. Push the strip of cardboard up through the cardboard tube and glue it in position.

2. Glue the triangles into the slits in the roll.

3. Finally put the stick inside the roll. Cut the rubber band, put the two ends through the two holes in the cardboard strip and tie knots to keep them in place. Stretch the rubber band up over the end of the stick.

Rocket

5, 4, 3, 2, 1—zero!
And you have lift-off! While
you count, pull the rubber
ring taut. At the word "zero"
let go. Your rocket will fly off
to the moon—or at least into
the back of your yard. Don't
worry if the rocket doesn't take
off perfectly the first time. That
can happen to big rockets too.

To make the pinwheels, you will need: some thick paper, wire, beads, wooden sticks, and paints and paintbrushes if you are going to paint them nice bright colors.

Cut your paper into squares of the same size with scissors. You will need one square for the single pinwheel and two squares for the double pinwheel. Fold the squares diagonally, and cut along the dotted lines as shown in the diagrams.

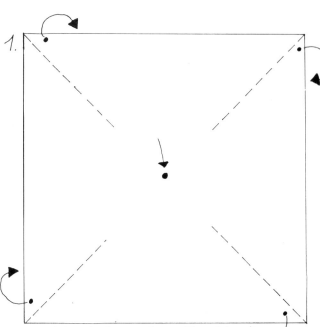

1.

With the paper lying in front of you like this, take the corners, bend them in to the center (see diagram above), and pin them down there.

2.

Double pinwheel
Section A

2.

Double pinwheel
Section B

For the double pinwheel, fit Sections A and B together as shown in the diagram below.

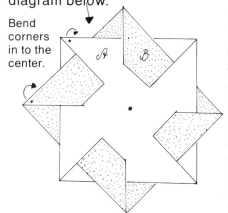

Bend corners in to the center.

Pin all corners together in the center with a fairly long piece of wire that has a bead on one end (twist the wire over to keep the bead in place).

When the pinwheel is threaded on the wire, put two more beads on the other side of the paper corners and wind the end of the wire around the wooden stick.

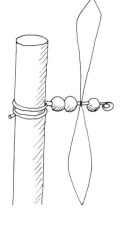

Pinwheels

These pinwheels will turn if you hold them in the wind or blow at them really hard. They are made of folded paper fastened to little sticks.

To make the windmill, you will need: a cardboard roll, some heavy cardboard, a wooden skewer, a very long piece of thin string, a thumbtack, scissors, glue, shiny paper, paints and a paintbrush.

1. Cut out a circle about 4 inches in diameter.

2. Make a single cut to the center of the circle.

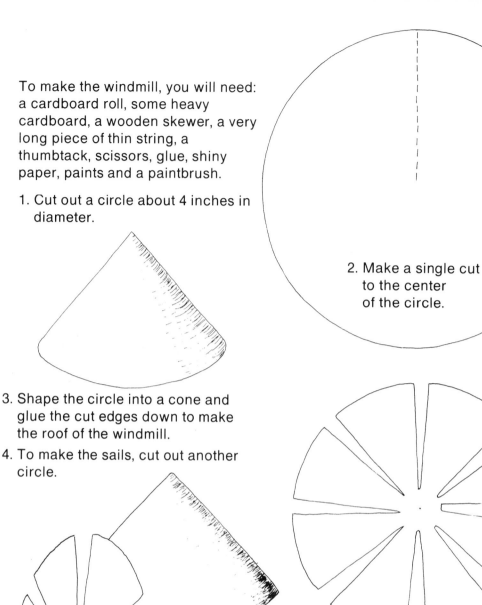

3. Shape the circle into a cone and glue the cut edges down to make the roof of the windmill.

4. To make the sails, cut out another circle.

5. Cut out the sails as shown in this diagram.

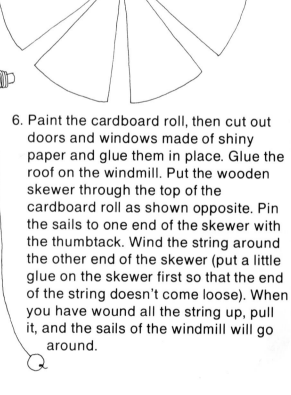

6. Paint the cardboard roll, then cut out doors and windows made of shiny paper and glue them in place. Glue the roof on the windmill. Put the wooden skewer through the top of the cardboard roll as shown opposite. Pin the sails to one end of the skewer with the thumbtack. Wind the string around the other end of the skewer (put a little glue on the skewer first so that the end of the string doesn't come loose). When you have wound all the string up, pull it, and the sails of the windmill will go around.

Windmill

You don't need any wind to turn the sails of this windmill—if you pull the string, they will go around. Make the windmill and try it for yourselves.

You will need:
scissors, glue, and
sheets of colored
paper (several
different colors).

1. First cut the paper
into strips.

2. Use two strips at once to
fold a "witch's staircase."
Place the strips together

as shown here, one on
top of the other. Glue
down the ends, and then
fold the strips alternately
over each other. Go on
until you reach the ends
of the strips. Glue these
two ends together as
well.

3. To make the head, cut a rectangle and
fold it along the dotted line. Then fold
again along the second set of dotted
lines.

Now the head will look like this. Take hold of
the corners of the paper bag you have made,
pull them apart, and . . .

. . . you will have a dragon's head.

Glue the head
to the body
here. ➡

Add eyes and eyelashes,
a tongue and teeth,
all cut out of
paper and stuck
in position,
and the dragon
is finished.

Dragon-Land

. . . is full of rustling and crackling and spitting and hissing when the dragons leave their caves. The Wizard of the Wood made them out of "witch's staircases"—you can make some dragons too. See opposite page for instructions.

To make the log cabin, you will
need: newspaper, glue, scissors,
and a pencil.

It will be more fun if you get some
friends to help you.

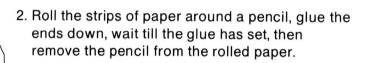

1. First cut a sheet of newspaper
   into strips.

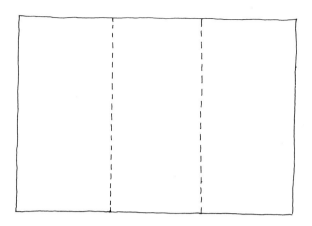

2. Roll the strips of paper around a pencil, glue the
   ends down, wait till the glue has set, then
   remove the pencil from the rolled paper.

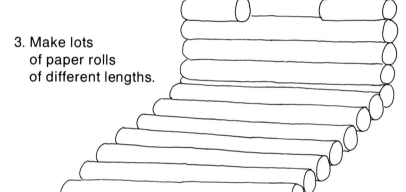

3. Make lots
   of paper rolls
   of different lengths.

4. Now glue enough paper
   rolls together to make
   the base of your house.
   Next, build the side
   walls, using short rolls
   of paper where you
   want to have doors or
   windows.

Fit rolls of paper together as shown here
and glue in place for the roof. Then glue
the roof on top of the house.

If you have any "logs" left over, you
can use them to make a fence.

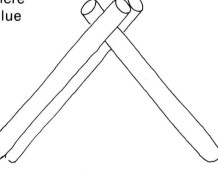

Log Cabin

This neat little log cabin is really made of rolled-up strips of newspaper. It won't stand up to the rain for long, but apart from that it's a solid little building.

It's easy to make these lanterns—
they are only cardboard cartons in
disguise.

To make them, you will need:
empty cartons, shoe boxes, egg
cartons, crepe paper, cardboard
tubes from toilet-paper rolls,
brushes and paints, wooden
sticks, wire, string, and small
flashlights.

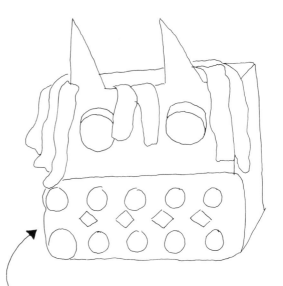

This monster is made out of a
carton open at the top. We glued
an egg carton on the face for a
mouth. If you bore holes in the
bottom of the egg carton, the
monster's mouth will shine. The
eyes are made of toilet-paper
tubes stuck in circular holes.
The monster's hair is made
of crepe paper, and it has
cardboard ears.

We did buy the basic lantern for
this one, but we added a bit of
extra disguise too. You might find
an old lantern that you could
decorate with paper hair, a paper
mouth, and paper eyes.

This fish lantern is quickly
made from a shoe box.
Cut holes in
the box for scales,
and stick colored
cellophane paper over the
holes on the inside
of the box.
Make the fish's head, fins, and tail of cardboard.

Bore holes in the box, put string
through them, and tie
the lantern to a stick.

Put a small
flashlight inside
each box and light it
when twilight falls.

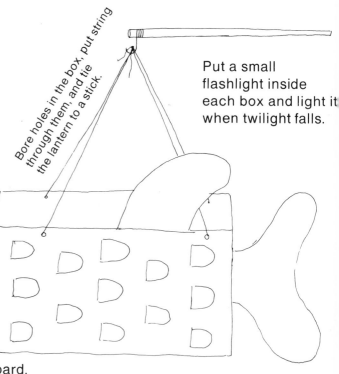

Halloween Lanterns

You can make your own Halloween lanterns out of cartons and boxes or cardboard. We made a fish out of a shoe box, a shining lion lantern, and a monster with egg-carton teeth. They look very good in the twilight. You could hang them up as decorations at a Halloween party.

To make these shining houses, you will need: white and fairly thin cardboard, wire, colored cellophane paper, scissors, glue, and wooden sticks, and small flashlights. Collect your materials before you start. The more of you there are, the bigger your town of shining houses will be.

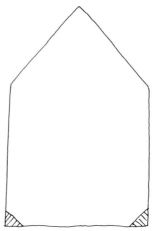

Draw a house-shaped pattern on cardboard and cut it out. Cut off the bottom corners.

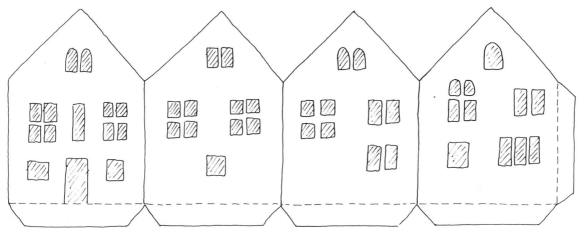

Using this shape as a pattern, draw four house shapes side by side on a long strip of white cardboard. Cut windows and doors in the house with scissors. Glue colored cellophane paper over the holes.

Cut out the whole outline of the four walls of the house with scissors. Bend the cardboard inward along the dotted lines. Fold the house into a square and glue it firmly together.

Now it will look like this:

Bore holes in the gables of the house.

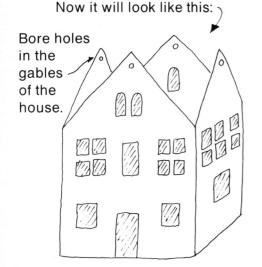

Cut a piece of cardboard to the right size for the floor of the house. Glue the floor to the walls.

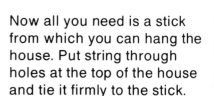

Now all you need is a stick from which you can hang the house. Put string through holes at the top of the house and tie it firmly to the stick.

When you have finished making the houses, put small flashlights inside them and light them after dark.

Shining Houses

These lanterns look like a pretty little town with lights inside the houses. You could tie them to sticks and carry them through the streets of your town.

To make the owl, you
will need:
a tall rectangular
carton, an egg carton,
stiff cardboard, paints
and a paintbrush, some
string, a few feathers,
and a small flashlight.

For the owl's head, cut
out a rectangle in the
front of the carton along
the dotted lines.
Use two sections of an
egg carton with the
pointed parts cut away
for the owl's eyes.

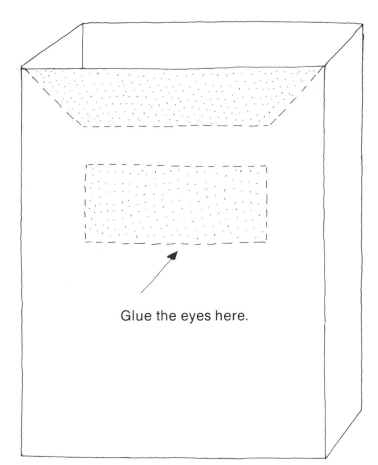

Glue the eyes here.

Follow this pattern
to cut out
the two
wings.

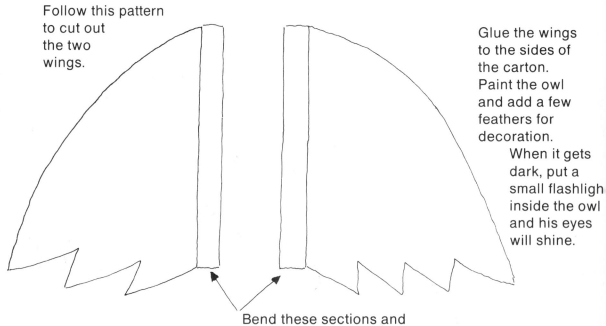

Glue the wings
to the sides of
the carton.
Paint the owl
and add a few
feathers for
decoration.
When it gets
dark, put a
small flashligh
inside the owl
and his eyes
will shine.

Bend these sections and
spread glue over them.

60

Owl Lantern

The owl's eyes shine in the dark—he looks almost like a real owl. You could carry this lantern around, or just hang it in a tree.

To make the dangling
animals, you will need
some fabric.
Cheesecloth is the most
suitable kind. It's cheap,
and you can paint it quite
easily. You will also need
scissors, a pencil, needle
and thread, stuffing for
the animals (kapok, or
old tights and stockings),
paints and a paintbrush.
Now you can begin.

1. Fold the fabric to a double
   thickness, draw an animal
   shape on it and cut the
   shape out.

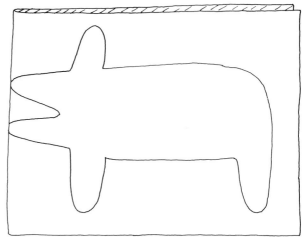

2. Stitch the animal
   together along the edges
   and turn it inside out.

Leave this section open.

3. Stuff the animal
   through the opening
   until it is fat enough.

4. Then sew up the open section.

5. Put string through the top of
   the animal (you might want
   to ask a grownup for help
   with this).

Paint the animal—and
if you are going to play
a game of throwing a
ball at the dangling
animals to score
points, don't forget to
paint numbers on the
sides.

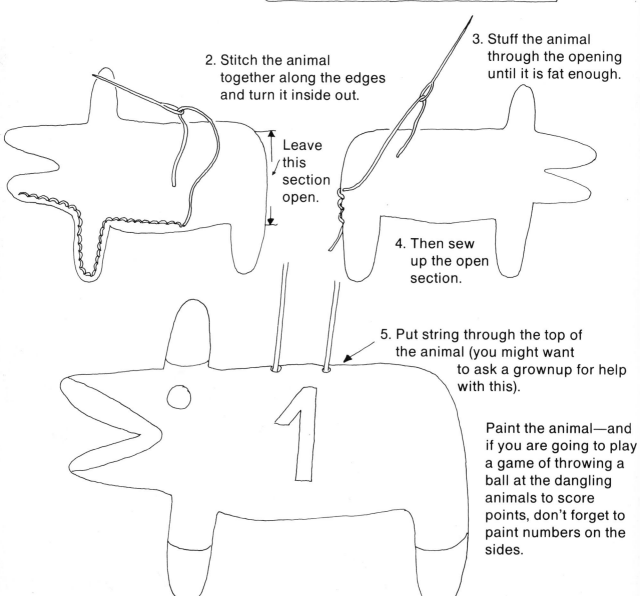

Danglers

You could play a point-scoring game by standing a little way from these dangling stuffed animals and throwing a ball at them. Invite your friends to come and compete. If each of you sewed one animal, you'd soon have quite a lot.

To make the shoe-box animals, you will need: empty shoe boxes, some stiff cardboard, scissors, glue, paints and paintbrushes, string, and a ball that will fit underneath a shoe box.

Decide what animals you are going to make out of the boxes. Cut extra parts of their bodies out of cardboard—e.g., ears, feet, hair, a snout, or whatever the animal may need.

To make the crocodile's snout, cut out two pieces of cardboard the same size, bend the sides in as shown here, and glue them together.

Feet

Ears

Cut a circle of cardboard for a mouth. Cut out the shaded section and glue the remaining part together at the edges.

Put a string through the animal's head and tie a knot inside the box.

Glue feet, ears, mouth, and tail on the shoe box and paint the animal a nice bright color.

Place a ball under the box, pick up the string, and then you can pull the animal along after you.

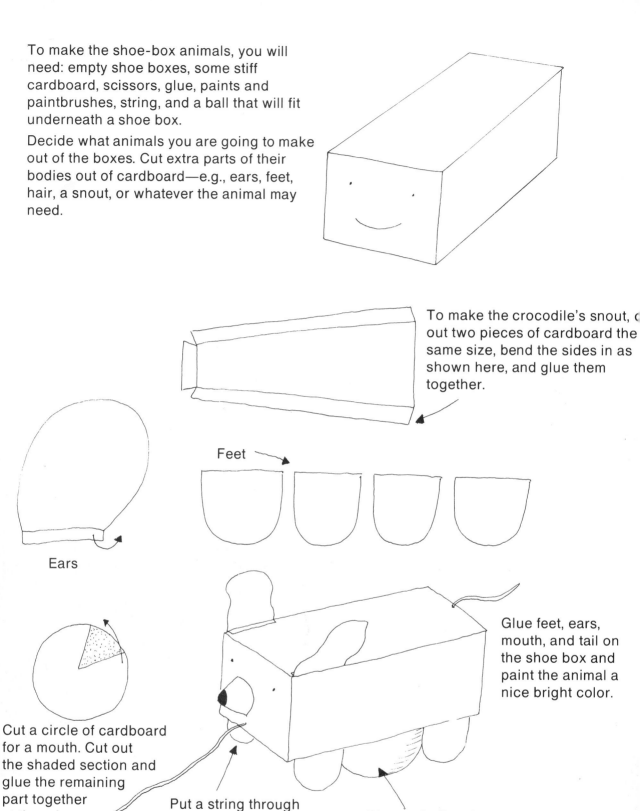

Shoe-Box Animals

You can use empty shoe boxes to make
crocodiles, lions, pigs, mice—all sorts of
animals. And if you put a ball underneath
the animals when you have made them,
you can even pull them along.

You will need: a large board, plenty of cardboard tubes big enough to take a marble, a knife, glue, paints and paintbrushes.

You can feed the marbles in anywhere the arrows point to start them rolling down their tracks.

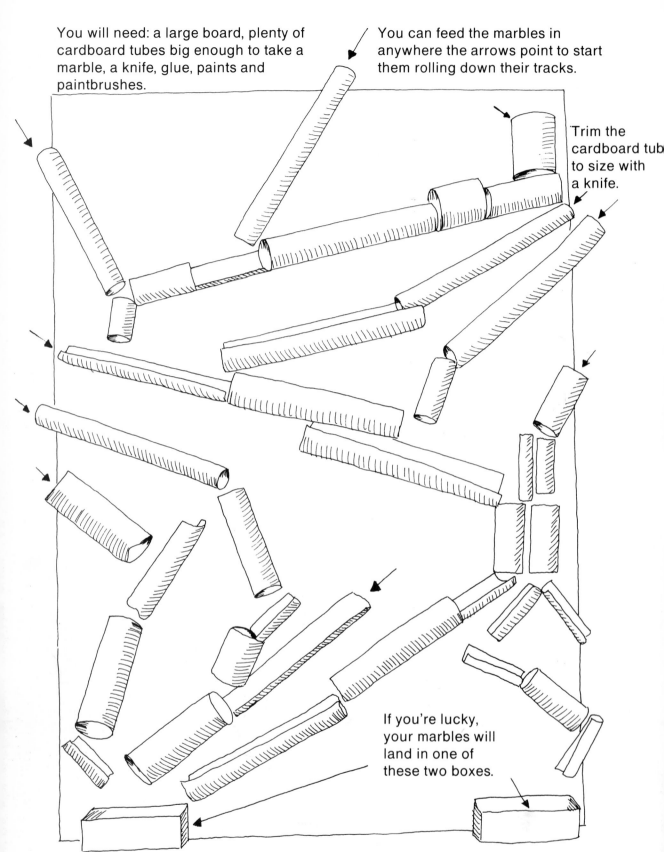

Trim the cardboard tube to size with a knife.

If you're lucky, your marbles will land in one of these two boxes.

It's easy to make the tracks for this marble game. Glue a lot of cardboard tubes to a board, roll marbles down the tubes, and see where they come out.

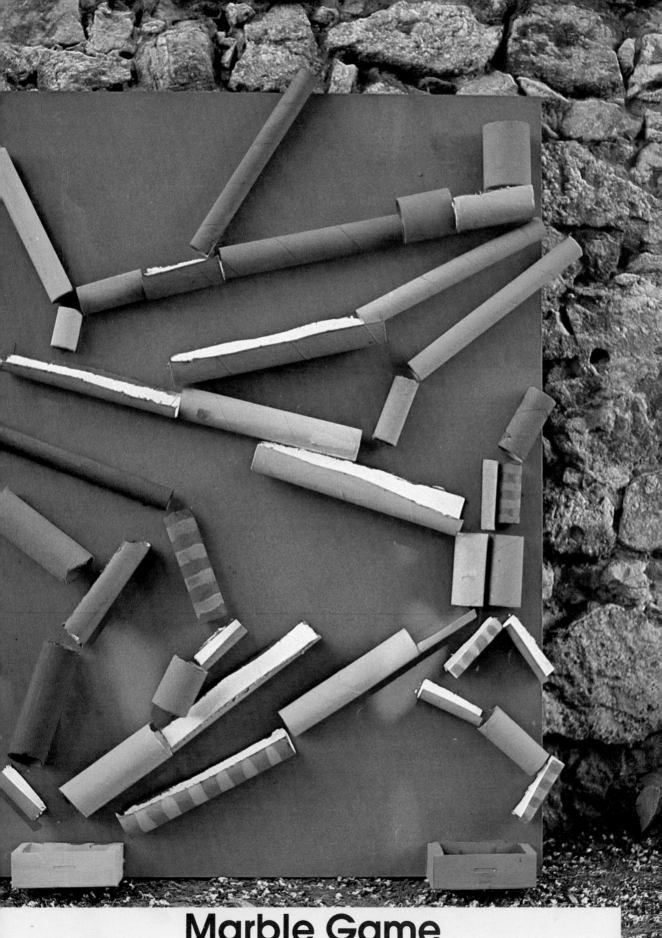

Marble Game

There are all sorts of ways to start marbles rolling down the tracks on the board. Will they fall off when they get to the bottom, or will they drop into one of the two boxes?

Its body is a big cardboard tube (the kind used for mailing things), cut in three parts. The nose and tail are made of cardboard tubes from paper-towel rolls, and the feet are made of the cardboard tubes from toilet-paper rolls.

The diagram shows you where to bore holes with a nail. Put strings through the holes. You can make the handles from which the strings hang out of sticks, or use puppets' string handles if available.

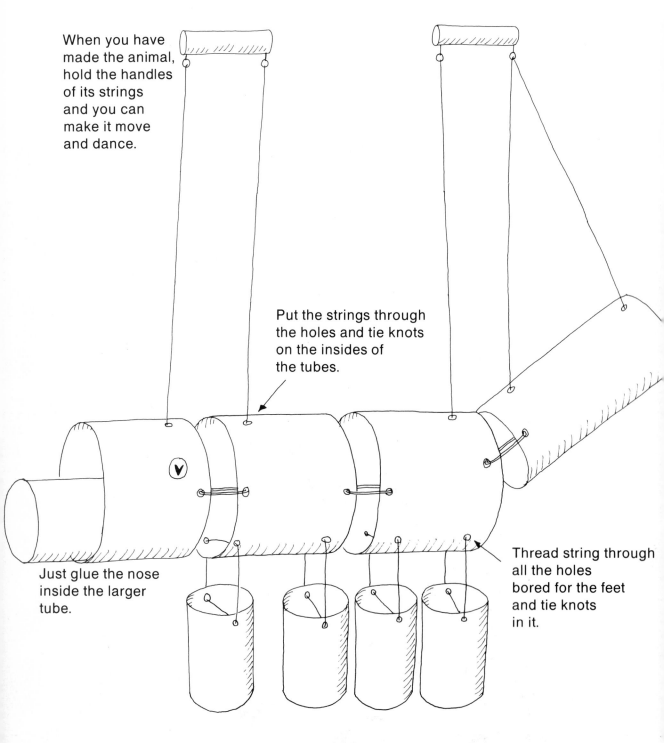

When you have made the animal, hold the handles of its strings and you can make it move and dance.

Put the strings through the holes and tie knots on the insides of the tubes.

Just glue the nose inside the larger tube.

Thread string through all the holes bored for the feet and tie knots in it.

68

Puppet Monster

"Spitfire" is the name of this terrible monster. It can wiggle its feet, head, tail, and body. Remember to hold its strings tight, or it might get away!

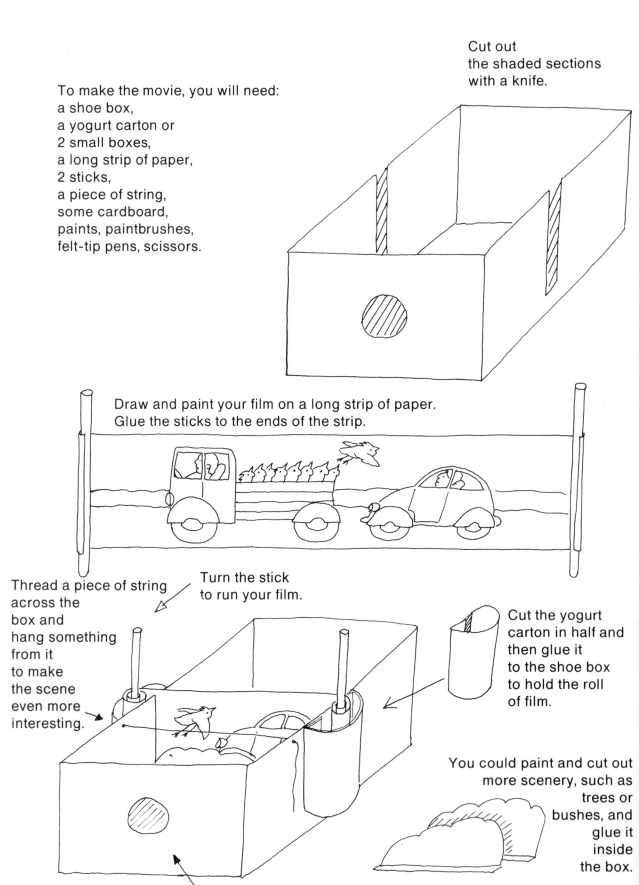

Cut out
the shaded sections
with a knife.

To make the movie, you will need:
a shoe box,
a yogurt carton or
2 small boxes,
a long strip of paper,
2 sticks,
a piece of string,
some cardboard,
paints, paintbrushes,
felt-tip pens, scissors.

Draw and paint your film on a long strip of paper.
Glue the sticks to the ends of the strip.

Thread a piece of string
across the
box and
hang something
from it
to make
the scene
even more
interesting.

Turn the stick
to run your film.

Cut the yogurt
carton in half and
then glue it
to the shoe box
to hold the roll
of film.

You could paint and cut out
more scenery, such as
trees or
bushes, and
glue it
inside
the box.

Look through this hole.

Shoe-Box Movie

A little painting, cutting out, and gluing—and you can invite your friends to your shoe-box movie. The film being shown in ours is about birds: one bird hangs from a string across the screen, and the film runs behind it, wound around two sticks by hand. You can probably think of lots of other ideas for films that you can draw and paint on strips of paper.

To make the Advent jigsaw puzzle, you will need: a sheet of paper large enough to take 24 matchboxes put side by side, paints and paintbrushes, glue, the 24 matchboxes, and 24 little surprises, such as candy, coins, little pictures, etc.

How to make the puzzle: paint a picture of Santa Claus or a Christmas tree on the sheet of paper. Then cut the paper into 24 rectangles and glue them to the matchboxes. Put a little surprise into each matchbox. You could give the puzzle to someone you're particularly fond of.

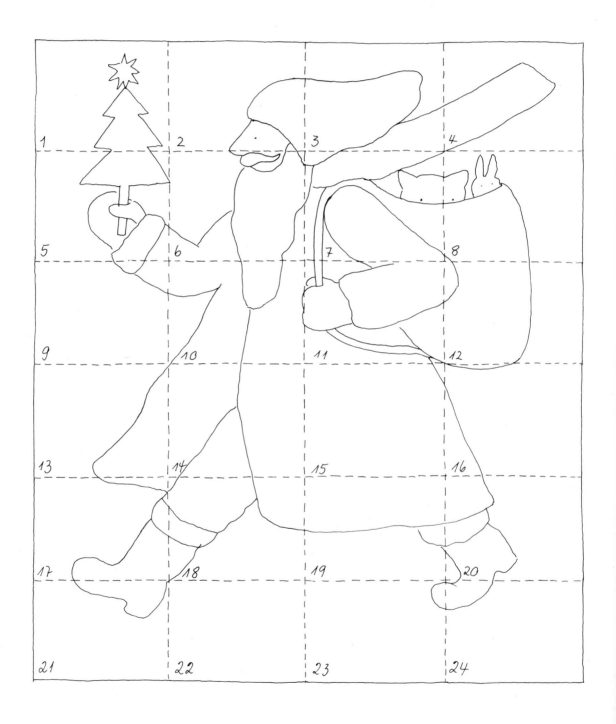

Advent Jigsaw Puzzle

You can make this jigsaw puzzle out of 24 matchboxes and a Christmas picture. Put candy or pictures and other little surprises inside the matchboxes. The puzzle would be a nice present to give a friend.

To make the bird, you will need: newspaper, paste, paints, paintbrushes, 2 balloons, crepe paper, a string, scissors, and some candy to put inside the bird when you have made it.

Newspaper

Paste

1. Stir the paste in the jar.

2. Blow up the balloons. You want one large balloon and one small one.

3. Spread paste over the newspaper and wrap it around the balloons, layer by layer. Make a beak at the front of the small balloon.

4. Stick the balloons together and wait until they are firmly stuck (leave them overnight if possible).

Put candy in here.

5. Cut a hole in the bird's back, and make two smaller holes. Put the string through the smaller holes.

6. Paint the bird and stick on wings and a tail made of crepe paper.

Piñata

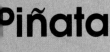

The people of Mexico sing and dance and have parties on the nights leading up to Christmas, and the children play a game called Piñata. A brightly colored papier-mâché animal filled with candy is hung up out-of-doors. Each child is blindfolded and tries to hit the animal with a stick so hard that it will burst open. When the candy falls to the ground, off comes the blindfold, and the children pick up as much candy as possible. Why not play Piñata yourselves?

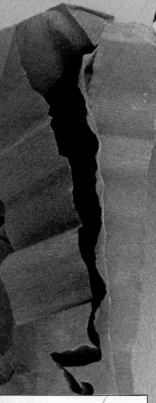

You need: paste, newspaper, crepe paper, paints, brushes, and two balloons.

Blow the balloons up and wrap three layers of newspaper around them. Spread paste on the newspaper first.

The smaller balloon is the head. Stick the head to the body and let the paste dry. You can run a pin through the newspaper to let the air out of the balloon.

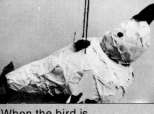

When the bird is completely dry, you can paint it. Cut an opening in the top of its body with your scissors, and fill it with candy.

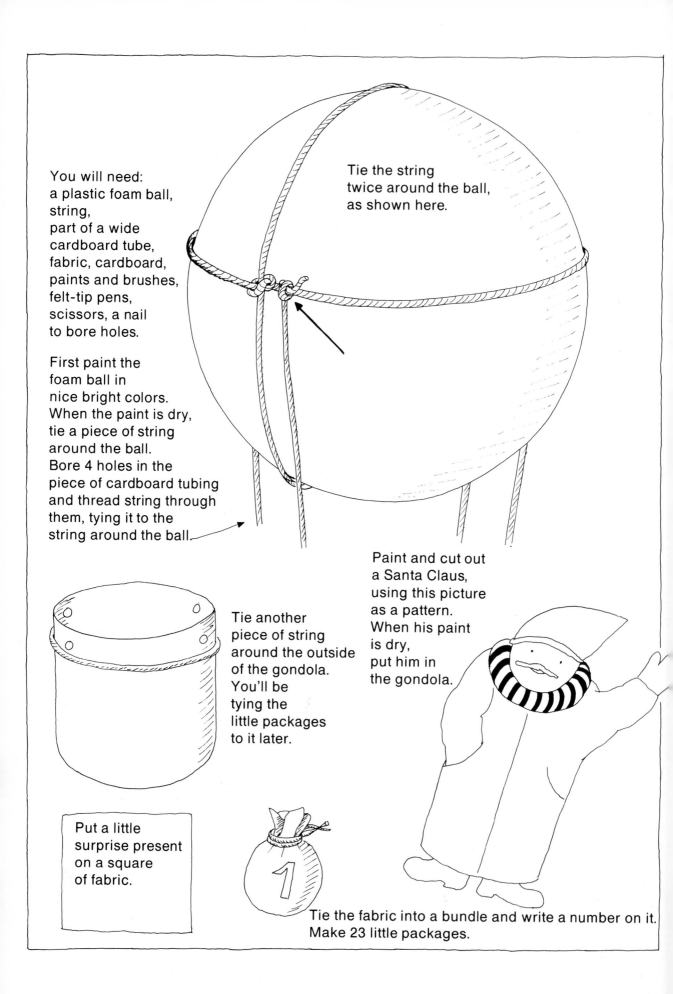

You will need:
a plastic foam ball,
string,
part of a wide
cardboard tube,
fabric, cardboard,
paints and brushes,
felt-tip pens,
scissors, a nail
to bore holes.

First paint the
foam ball in
nice bright colors.
When the paint is dry,
tie a piece of string
around the ball.
Bore 4 holes in the
piece of cardboard tubing
and thread string through
them, tying it to the
string around the ball.

Tie the string
twice around the ball,
as shown here.

Tie another
piece of string
around the outside
of the gondola.
You'll be
tying the
little packages
to it later.

Paint and cut out
a Santa Claus,
using this picture
as a pattern.
When his paint
is dry,
put him in
the gondola.

Put a little
surprise present
on a square
of fabric.

Tie the fabric into a bundle and write a number on it.
Make 23 little packages.

Advent Balloon

Santa Claus comes
flying to see you in a
balloon, for a change.
The ballast of the
balloon is made of
little surprise presents
—open one a day
until Christmas Eve,
December 24th, when
the balloon lands, and
Christmas has arrived.

To make the penguins, you will need black and white cardboard, the cardboard tubes from toilet-paper rolls, glue, paints and brushes.

Use polystyrene packaging material for the snowy landscape.

To make a complete set of penguins for Advent, you will need 23. For the 24th day, use an igloo made of pieces of polystyrene.

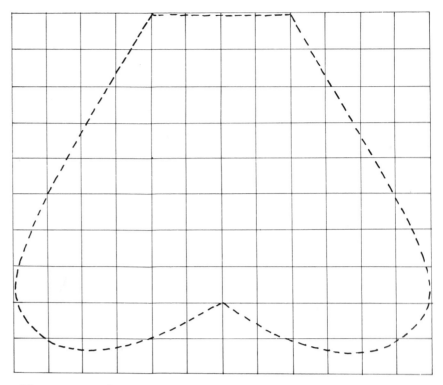

First cut out the wings, following this pattern.

Then cut out the feet.

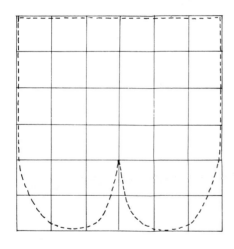

Cut out this shape
for the beak
and fold it
in the middle.

Paint the toilet-paper roll white, glue on the feet and wings, paint the penguin's eyes, glue on a yellow beak, and the penguin is ready. If you are making a complete set of Advent penguins, paint a number on the body and put a little surprise present inside it.

78

Penguin Family

Why not make a model of a snowy landscape with 23 penguins and an igloo for Advent? Put 24 little surprises inside the penguins and the igloo—the best one in the igloo. Take one out each day until Christmas.

INDEX